LET'S DANCE!

TAP

by Joyce Markovics

CHERRY LAKE PRESS
Ann Arbor, Michigan

Cherry Lake Press

Published in the United States of America by
Cherry Lake Publishing Group
Ann Arbor, Michigan
www.cherrylakepublishing.com

Reading Adviser: Beth Walker Gambro, MS Ed., Reading Consultant, Yorkville, IL

Content Adviser: Justin Wingenroth, dancer and owner/director of The Dance Conservatory, Cortland Manor, New York

Book Designer: Ed Morgan, Bowerbird Books

Photo Credits: © Evan Hurd/dance and movement/Alamy Stock Photo, cover and title page; freepik.com, 5; © AMA/Shutterstock, 6; © 2017 Kathy Hutchins/Hutchins Photo/Newscom, 7; © Antonio Pagano/Photoshot/Newscom, 8–9; Wikimedia Commons, 10, 11, 13, 15, 16, 17 top and bottom, and 20; Library of Congress, Music Division, 14; Photographer-James Kriegsmann, New York/Wikimedia Commons, 18; Library of Congress, Prints and Photographs Division, Van Vechten Collection,19; © JASON TENCH/Shutterstock, 21; © COLUMBIA PICTURES/Album/Newscom, 22; © BILL HOGAN/KRT/Newscom, 23; © Stephen Smith/Sipa USA/Newscom, 24; © Pablo Serrano Huguet/Shutterstock, 25; © Rus S/Shutterstock, 26–27.

Cherry Lake Press is an imprint of Cherry Lake Publishing Group.

Library of Congress Cataloging-in-Publication Data has been filed and is available at catalog.loc.gov

Printed in the United States of America

Contents

It's Showtime! 4
What Is Tap? 6
A Brief History 10
Famous Tappers 18
Get Moving! 24
Learn to Dance 28
Glossary 30
Read More 31
Learn More Online 31
Index 32
About the Author 32

It's SHOWTIME!

"Tap is the dance of creating music."
—Michelle Dorrance

A flood of sounds pours from the stage. Some tones are gentle and soft. Others are deep and rich. Together, all of the sounds create music. But the music isn't coming from an orchestra or band. It's coming from the metal plates, or taps, on a dancer's shoes! The dancer strikes her toe and heel taps on the floor. The sound is like a drumbeat. *Boom, boom, bah!* Creating a bouncy rhythm, the dancer shuffles. Then she slides across the stage as a skater would. After, she leaps and spins in a dazzling display. Her arms gracefully rise and fall. The audience excitedly watches and listens.

A tap dancer hits the floor with her taps in different ways. Each strike creates a unique sound.

What Is TAP?

"It's like a soaring kind of dance, there's no limit to what you can do with it."
—Suzanne Douglas

Most dancers dance to music. Tap dancers, or tappers, *create* the music. "The body becomes music," said Michelle Dorrance. She is a tap dancer, teacher, and **choreographer** with her own dance company. "There's not a time I can remember when I wasn't in love with tap dancing," Michelle said. "It's part of who I am."

Michelle is one of the most respected tap dancers in the world. Tap wouldn't be what it is today without people like her. But she says, "You must constantly educate about the past." Throughout history, Michelle and countless others, especially Black dancers, have helped create and shape tap into the art form it is.

Tap dancer Michelle Dorrance

Michelle Dorrance grew up learning ballet, **jazz**, and tap. Each dance style helped her become better at tap.

Did you know that dance is one of the oldest art forms? The ancient Egyptians danced, as did other early peoples. Today, dance exists in most **cultures** around the world. But dancing is more than moving—or learning steps—to music. Dancing expresses ideas! People dance to tell stories and show their feelings. They dance to celebrate happy times and **mourn** losses. Whether performer or audience member, dance, such as tap, brings people together.

What makes tap dancing extra unique is not just the metal heel and toe taps. Tap dancing is an American dance story. It reflects our history, who we are, and where we're going. Let's dance!

Master tap dancers Savion Glover (left) and Marshall Davis Jr. (right) performing

A Brief History

"It's like a bird flying here and flying there, flying everywhere."
—Sandman Sims

Although tap is an American dance, it has roots in other cultures. Experts say an African dance called *gioube*, or juba, inspired tap. Gioube involved a circle of dancers bent at the waist. They stomped, clapped, and patted the body to drumbeats. People danced the gioube as a community to mark life experiences. When West Africans were enslaved and shipped to the **Caribbean** and North America starting in the 1500s, they brought gioube with them.

In the past, clogging was called "shoe music." When people clog, their upper bodies stay motionless.

Similarly, Irish people had their own stepping dances. These were clog dances, hornpipes, and jigs commonly performed to fiddle music. All included a rhythmic beating of the feet. In the 1600s, many poor Irish people were **deported** to the Caribbean. Once there, they worked as **indentured servants** on **plantations**. Often, they were side by side with enslaved Africans.

Sailors performing the hornpipe

The hornpipe can include several dances performed in hard shoes. In some hornpipes, the feet move so fast that they tap 70 times in 15 seconds!

It wasn't uncommon for the Africans and Irish to work and live together. "For an entire century, these two peoples are left out in the fields . . . to grow into something new," said dance expert and historian Leni Sloan. The Africans learned to play fiddles. And the Irish drums. The two groups shared their cultures. And, many times, they danced as one.

This cultural exchange continued as millions of enslaved Africans were brought to mainland America. To keep a connection to their culture and each other, they danced to drum music. Then, in 1739, a group of enslaved South Carolinians rose up to fight for their freedom. They were captured and killed. Afterward, enslavers passed new laws to control enslaved people. The beating of drums was outlawed. Yet even without drums, the enslaved people found a way to express themselves, find joy, and make rhythms—with only their bare feet.

This 1780s painting shows enslaved African Americans dancing on a plantation, which they did to express joy, hope, resistance, sadness, and grief. However, it does not show the cruelty and abuse they faced.

The dance form that developed was called jigging. To perform it, dancers rapidly moved their lower body and shuffled their feet. Soon, there were jigging competitions on plantations. Born around 1850, James W. Smith was enslaved in Texas. He remembers seeing a fellow enslaved person making "his feet go like triphammers and sound like the snare drum."

This early print shows people jigging.

In the 1800s, white Americans created minstrel shows. These shows spread racist **stereotypes**. The performers, who were often white, painted their faces black to mock Black people. The shows featured music and dance, especially jigging. Black and white dancers alike showed off their skills during dance battles later called "cutting contests." They shuffled and slid across the stage, stomped, jumped, and kicked. Excited audiences cheered on their favorite dancers.

A portrait of Master Juba

One of the most famous Black minstrel show dancers was known as Master Juba. He challenged and beat the best white dancers of the day.

Tap as we know it was born decades later. In the 1920s, dancers attached metal plates to the bottoms of their shoes. These "taps" made their steps louder. As tap dancing developed, so did the music people danced to. It was called jazz. Jazz and tap reached new heights with *Shuffle Along*. It was a jazz tap **Broadway** musical. The show became a huge hit and launched the careers of Josephine Baker and Florence Mills. It also helped tap become popular from Broadway to Hollywood.

This is a poster from the musical *Shuffle Along*.

From the 1920s on, most shows featured tap dancers. In fact, it was hard for performers to get jobs if they didn't know how to tap dance. During this time, many tap dancers rose to fame. As they danced across America, they added new steps, rhythms, and energy to tap.

Born in 1896, Florence Mills was a talented singer and tap dancer. She was nicknamed the "Queen of Happiness."

Josephine Baker was a famous dancer, singer, and actress. In 1927, she was the first Black woman to star in a major motion picture.

Famous Tappers

"Listen to my feet and I will tell you the story of my life."
—John Sublett "Bubbles"

There were many outstanding tappers from the 1920s to the 1950s. One of the best was Bill "Bojangles" Robinson. As a child, he danced for pennies in the street. When he got older, he worked in **vaudeville**. Soon, he was a headliner. Bill was known especially for his "Stair Dance." Using precise and complex footwork, he rhythmically tapped up and down a flight of stairs. The famous writer Langston Hughes called the show "human **percussion**." Using his own **ingenuity**, Bill created something entirely new. Yet he still held onto his African **heritage**.

Bill "Bojangles" Robinson was one of the most highly paid Black entertainers of his day. He shared the stage with Shirley Temple, who tapped at 6 years old.

Another great tap dancer was John Sublett, known as "Bubbles." He performed with Ford Lee "Buck" Washington in an act called "Buck and Bubbles." John used his heels to bring fresh rhythms to tap. He also created original and exciting moves. "If I got four shows, I'd do it four different ways," he said. "I never did the same step the same way."

John Sublett "Bubbles"

Many of the best tap dancers performed at the Hoofers Club in Harlem, New York. "You could hear dancing the minute you got in the building," said a tap dancer who performed at the club.

Bill Robinson's and John Sublett's tapping influenced a young Eleanor Powell. As a child, Eleanor studied ballet and **acrobatics**. Then she got a taste for tap and quickly made a name for herself. Eleanor's tap dancing was fast and powerful yet smooth and graceful. Soon, she was known as "the world's greatest female tap dancer." Eleanor starred in several Hollywood films. She teamed up with Fred Astaire in one. A **versatile** dancer, Fred combined tap with other styles. He made tap look as easy as a walk in the park. He shined as a **soloist** and also as a partner dancer in many films.

Eleanor Powell

Apart from Fred, one of the most unique tap dancers was Clayton "Peg Leg" Bates. When he was 12, he lost his leg in a farming accident. Clayton then wore a wooden leg, attached taps to it, and taught himself to dance. He wowed audiences across the country with his **inventive** tapping.

Here's a statue of Clayton "Peg Leg" Bates in South Carolina. He frequently performed for other people with disabilities.

The Nicholas Brothers were tappers who appeared in more than 50 Hollywood movies! This self-taught **dynamic** pair were known for their speed, skill, and striking steps.

In the 1950s, tap dancing became less popular. Then in the 1960s and 1970s, tap gained attention again. Broadway shows that showcased tap lit up the stage. These included *42nd Street* and *Black and Blue*. A standout tapper, Gregory Hines, first appeared in the musical *Eubie*. Then he stole the spotlight in *Jelly's Last Jam*. Fans were struck by his elegance and confidence. Gregory also starred in movies, including *White Nights* where he danced alongside the ballet great Mikhail Baryshnikov.

Gregory Hines sailing above the dance floor in the movie *White Nights*

While Gregory was sharing his talent with the world, a young Savion Glover was making his **debut**. At 10 years old, Savion starred in *The Tap Dance Kid*. His footwork was fast, precise, and **innovative**. Before long, he was dancing alongside Gregory. He also began teaching and choreographing tap. In 1995, Savion created and starred in *Bring in 'da Noise, Bring in 'da Funk*. The show used rap and tap to talk about Black history. It won many awards. People flocked to see it. Tap has been in the limelight ever since.

Savion Glover calls his unique style of tap "hitting."

Tap dancers use their shoes as instruments, creating different notes with their feet. To make the clearest sounds, dancers use their entire bodies, especially their knees, ankles, and feet.

Get Moving!

"I believe that tap is magic."
—Ayodele Casel

Thanks to Gregory, Savion, and the many dancers who came before them, tap is a celebrated art form today. Today's tappers divide tap into two main groups: theatrical and rhythm. Theatrical dancers often use traditional steps from the past and dance to music. While rhythm tappers, like Savion and Ayodele Casel, use their feet to make music. Raised in Puerto Rico and the Bronx, Ayodele loves to bring people together through dance. "Rhythm is something everyone can connect with," she said.

Ayodele Casel is a tapper and teacher.

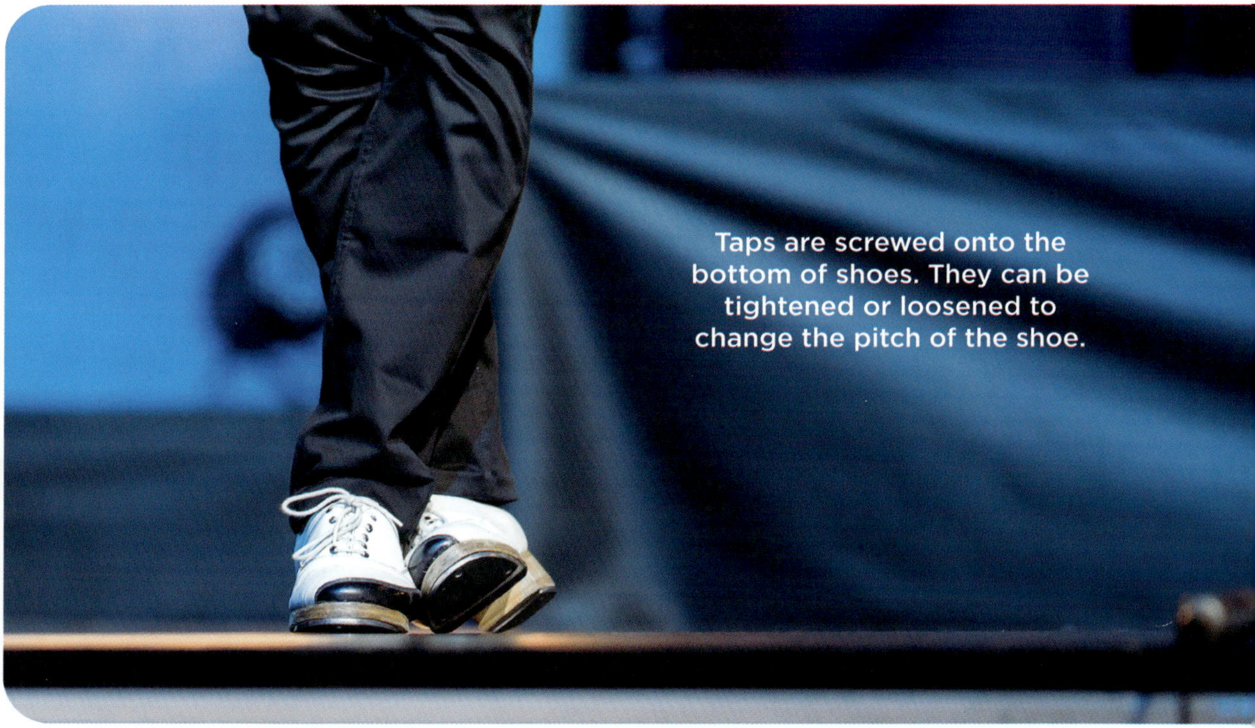

Taps are screwed onto the bottom of shoes. They can be tightened or loosened to change the pitch of the shoe.

Caleb Teicher, a **non-binary** tapper with lightning-quick feet, started with Michelle Dorrance's dance company. Then they formed their own. They collaborate with different musicians from **beatboxers** to pianists. Because tap is an art form, it can be interpreted in many ways. So, Caleb puts their own spin on it. "It is the way in which I process the world," they said.

"What success I achieved in the theatre is due to the fact that I have always worked just as hard when there were ten people in the house as when there were thousands."
—Bill "Bojangles" Robinson

Every time a tapper dances, they're sharing the history of the art form. They're also telling their own story! How can you join in? You can be a part of the tradition by seeing a tap performance or by learning how to tap. Taking classes is a great way to experience tap. You will learn something new as well as express yourself. In addition to that, dancingDancing helps you stay fit and connect with other people. As a famous dancer once said, "Great dancers are not great because of their **technique**, they are great because of their passion." So get out there, get moving—and let's dance!

Learn to DANCE

Here are steps to learn a basic tap dance move called the shuffle. It's a combination of two simpler moves, the brush and spank.

Step 1: Stand with your feet parallel and about as wide as your hips.

Step 2: Bend your knees slightly but not too much so that they go past your toes. Always keep your knees slightly bent when tap dancing.

Step 3: To perform the brush, stand on one leg and bend the other as you lift your foot off the ground.

Step 4: Swing the foot forward to perform the brush. As it passes your standing foot, extend your knee so the ball of your foot quickly brushes against the floor. Don't let your heel touch the floor.

Step 5: Perform a spank. This is the same movement in reverse. Swing your foot backward instead of forward.

Congrats, you just performed a shuffle!

Glossary

acrobatics (ak-ruh-BAT-iks) spectacular gymnastic moves

beatboxers (BEAT-box-uhrz) people who use their voices to sound like drums or other sounds

Broadway (BRAWD-way) a street in New York City famous for its theaters and show business

Caribbean (kuh-RIB-ee-uhn) having to do with the Caribbean Sea and its islands, located between North and South America

choreographer (kor-ee-AWG-ruh-fer) a person who creates the steps and moves for a dance performance

cultures (KUHL-churz) the customs, ideas, art, and traditions that make up people's ways of life

debut (day-BYOO) to appear for the first time

deported (dih-PORT-uhd) sent away to another country

dynamic (dye-NAM-ik) energetic and powerful

heritage (HAIR-ih-tij) qualities or traditions that have been passed down from previous generations

indentured servants (in-DEN-cherd SUR-vuhnts) people who are forced to work without pay for a set number of years

ingenuity (in-juh-NOO-ih-tee) the quality of being clever, original, and creative

innovative (in-uh-VAY-tiv) having new ideas about how something can be done

inventive (in-VEN-tiv) the ability to create or design new things

jazz (JAZ) a type of dance, usually performed to jazz or other upbeat music

mourn (MORN) to feel very sad about someone who has died

non-binary (NON-bahy-nuh-ree) refers to a person who does not identify as a man or a woman

percussion (per-KUHSH-uhn) refers to musical instruments that include drums, cymbals, gongs, bells, and rattles

stereotypes (STAIR-ee-uh-tahyps) widely held but oversimplified views about certain groups of people

technique (tek-NEEK) a skillful way of doing something

vaudeville (VAWD-vil) a style of entertainment that was popular in the United States from the 1880s to the early 1930s and featured a variety of acts in each show

versatile (VUR-suh-tuhl) useful in many ways

Read More

BOOKS

Lanier, Wendy Hinote. *Tap Dance*. Lake Elmo, MN: Focus Readers, 2017.

Rissman, Rebecca. *Today's Tap Dancing*. Minneapolis, MN: Capstone Press, 2019.

Rooyackers, Paul. *101 Dance Games for Children*. Alameda, CA: Hunter House Publishing, 1996.

Learn More Online

WEBSITES

Explore these online sources with an adult:

Britannica Kids: Savion Glover

New York Stage Originals: Tap Kids Study Guide

University Musical Society: A Brief Tap Dance History

Index

African dance, 10
Astaire, Fred, 20
Baker, Josephine, 16–17
Bates, Clayton "Peg Leg," 21
Broadway, 16, 22
Caribbean plantations, 10–12
Casel, Ayodele, 24
choreography, 6, 23
cutting contests, 15
Dorrance, Michelle, 6–7
gioube (juba), 10
Glover, Savion, 23
Hines, Gregory, 22-23
Hoofers' Club, 19
hornpipe, 11
Irish dance, 11
jazz, 16
jigging, 14–15
Master Juba, 15
Mills, Florence, 16–17
minstrel shows, 15
Nicholas Brothers, 21
Powell, Eleanor, 20
racist stereotypes, 15
Robinson, Bill "Bojangles," 18
Shuffle Along, 16
slavery, 10–14
Sloan, Leni, 12
Sublett, John "Bubbles," 19
tap
  benefits of, 26
  dance history, 8
  history of, 10–17
  learning, 26, 28–29
  styles of, 24
  using the body in, 23
taps, 4–5, 16, 21, 25
Teicher, Caleb, 25
Washington, Ford Lee "Buck," 19

About the Author

Joyce Markovics has written hundreds of children's books. She wholeheartedly thanks Justin Wingenroth for his expert help with this series. Joyce and Justin urge everyone to get up and dance!